Breadcrumbs &Seeds

Revised Edition

Isabel Malvenia Collins

authorHOUSE®

AuthorHouse™
1663 Liberty Drive
Bloomington, IN 47403
www.authorhouse.com
Phone: 833-262-8899

As you read this book, I pray that you will focus on finding yourself in my faith walk rather than trying to figure out the missing pieces that I do not mention. It only covers information that I was led to share, and it is not for gossiping, judging, or condemning.

All Scripture quotations, unless otherwise indicated, are taken from King James Bible App Version 3.41.0. Offered by Ozion. Updated on Jan 30, 2024. Released on Jan 2, 2018. All rights reserved.

Photograph taken by Joe W Collins Jr. and used with his permission.

Published by AuthorHouse 01/15/2025

ISBN: 979-8-8230-3879-9 (sc)
ISBN: 979-8-8230-3880-5 (e)

Library of Congress Control Number: 2024926145

Print information available on the last page.

DEDICATION

This book is dedicated to my family, for loving me even when I was not my best self, to those who were used by God to pour into me, and to the countless others whose lives have crossed my path or will one day.

Some Favorite Scriptures
Jeremiah 29:11
Psalms 4, 23, 27, 51, 91
Romans 12
Proverbs 3
Psalms 139:1-18; 23-24

CONTENTS

ACKNOWLEDGMENT

I give all the glory and honor to our Father in Heaven for this book is a testimony to how He saved a wretch like me throughout many seasons of my life.

I express my appreciation to the many churches and pastors from whom I have learned, and who have poured into me wisdom, knowledge, and understanding of the Bible, the living word of God.

To Melanie Lear and the rest of the AuthorHouse Publishing team thank you for your patience and kindness while working with me as a client to get this book published. I could not have done it without you.

INTRODUCTION

I have written these pages in hopes that some people will be encouraged as they read them. I hope that their faith becomes renewed in Jesus Christ, our Lord, and Savior. See, maybe you haven't experienced what God can do for yourself, so you need to live vicariously through someone else's experiences until you have your own experiences with God, who is the Alpha and the Omega, the Beginning and the End, I Am Who I Am. Thus, these pages I write for you. Some experiences may seem small; others may seem big. Whatever you take from them, know that nothing is too small or big for our God to handle.

REFERENCE SCRIPTURES

❖ Ephesians 3:19-21 And to know the love of Christ, which passeth knowledge, that ye might be filled with all the fulness of God. Now unto him that is able to do exceeding abundantly above all that we ask or think. According to the power that worketh in us, Unto him be glory in the church by Christ Jesus throughout all ages, world without end.
Amen.

❖ Jeremiah 32:17 Ah Lord GOD! Behold, thou hast made the heaven and the earth by thy great power and stretched out arm, and there is nothing too hard for thee.

CHAPTER 1

Weary in Doing Good

SOME YEARS HAD passed. I was in a state of loneliness, anxiety, and depression. I had begun to let every little thing offend me. I knew I needed to get rid of something or someone, but just did not know what or who. Since I did not know who or what, I started with me getting rid of the dishes, pots, and pans.

I stopped cooking and cleaning, cleaning and cooking. I felt that no one in the household was helping me, so I would just stop doing what began to overwhelm me. Along with work and school demands, all the menial tasks at home seemed big. Something had to be done, so I stopped, just stopped doing things in the house that others could do but would not, even after I stopped.

At this time in my life, I was not rooted and grounded in Christ, as I am now. I did not have a prayer life or a church home. I did not have many people in my life who were Christ-centered themselves. I mean true believers who did not waver. I watched as they appeared to have it together; however, they were being pulled back and forth, like me, lukewarm, neither hot nor cold.

After years of vacillating with my belief in God, a day came during the season of the Pandemic when I was in the grocery store. While there, I came upon a man shopping for his father. I decided to speak. He spoke back. We had a conversation discussing how tired we were from doing for others and not much for our own wellbeing. On this day, I did not realize that this man had provided a breadcrumb, that he planted a seed that would later be revealed to me as a message from God.

"Don't be weary in doing good," he said. I do not know if he had known that he had provided me with such an encounter from God, or maybe he did. Either way, those words became a flicker to a flame that ignited a fire for me to yearn for understanding.

When I returned home, I googled the words and found that they were from a scripture in the Bible. I opened my Bible and found the scripture verse. As I read it, I reflected on the words.

I looked over my life up to that point and related the text to myself. That is it! I had become weary in doing good. I did not remember to take my burdens to the One who can bear them. I had lost my way, and right there in the grocery store, God gave me a word to begin my journey back to having a relationship with Him, in Christ

Heavenly Father, I do not even remember if I thanked you for that day. Please forgive me. I take this moment to say thank you for bringing me back to you, the One who knows my name and all about me. Thank you for saving a wretch like me. I am ever so grateful. In Jesus' name, I pray. Amen.

REFERENCE SCRIPTURES

- ❖ Galatians 6:9 And let us not be weary in well doing: for in due season we shall reap, if we faint not.
- ❖ 2 Thessalonians 3:13- But ye, Brethen, be not weary in well doing.
- ❖ Matthew 11:28-30 Come unto me, all ye that labour and are heavy laden, and I will give you rest. Take my yoke upon you, and learn of me; for I am meek and lowly in heart: and ye shall find rest unto your souls. For my yoke is easy, and my burden is light.

SELF-REFLECTION

Questions to ask yourself:

1. Think of a time when you became weary and tired in doing good, how did you feel? What did you do to feel better about the circumstances?

2. What would you consider to be good?

3. What do you believe that Jesus what do or say concerning good and weariness?

_____

_____

_____

_____

_____

_____

_____

_____

_____

_____

CHAPTER 2

In a Ditch

HAVE YOU EVER been so giving and generous that you gave what you did not even have to give? You borrowed from "Peter to pay Paul," as the saying goes. Well, that is what I did. No matter who asked or gave a story about their need, there I would be to help in whatever way I could. People knew it too, so they would eat it up. Oh, how foolish I was. No discernment or understanding about the blind leading the blind; then they both fall into a ditch.

"I want you to know what I learned about myself during this time in a ditch." I gave because I thought it was a way to receive love. I gave because of my God-given gift of helps and giving. I also gave because I believed I had to buy others' love if I wanted them to love me or even like me. Then when I had nothing else to give, guess what happened? Yes, I fell into a ditch. No, not a literal ditch, if you are wondering. I was in debt. There was no rainy day savings because it was exhausted from previous rainy days. Credit cards were maxed or over the limit. Not to mention my student loan debt from going to college to obtain a master's degree.

Here I am in what appears to be a ditch, and everyone disappeared. They ran away, left my life, just like that. The well ran dry. Because I had nothing else to give or to offer, as it appeared, no one wanted to be bothered when I called them. Additionally, they would not call me because as I had already informed them, I was tapped out. There were no more invites for going out to eat or watch a movie. No more hair or nail salon visits. I was left with no one to call upon for help or, as others would say, my pride set in.

Then one day, sometime after my prayer asking God to take my five loaves of bread and two fish (my paycheck, of course) and make it enough, I was given another crumb or a seed, per se, to help me become learned in how to become a better steward over what God has already provided. Hence, the Bible verse I quoted earlier, Matthew 15:14, "Let them alone; they be blind leaders of the blind. And if the blind lead the blind, both shall fall into the ditch." This was another encounter with God from the word. An "Aha" moment.

He taught me that love does not cost anything. You see, we love because He first loved us. He sacrificed His son for our sins and so that we could be saved. Jesus paid the price already for us. What an awesome God to serve. One that loves and teaches us how to love.

God showed me that I do not have to always give money or monetary things. What He has given me is worth more than silver and gold. He set me in a place to begin again. To learn how to become a better steward over what He has blessed me with. To give unto Him, first. Then to my household and others.

Therefore, to honor God for what He has done and is doing in my life for His glory, I write to tell others of His goodness, kindness, grace, and mercy. Moreover, to say, if He did it for me, He surely can do it for you. Glory to our King. A victory won, in Jesus' name.

REFERENCE SCRIPTURES

❖ 1 John 4:19 We love him, because He first loved us

❖ Matthew 15:14 Let them alone: they be blind leaders of the blind. And if the blind lead the blind, both shall fall into the ditch.

❖ Proverbs 3:13-17 Happy is the man that findeth wisdom, and the man that getteth understanding. For the merchandise of it is better than the merchandise of silver, and the gain thereof than fine gold. She is more precious than rubies: and all the things thou canst desire are not to be compared unto her. Length of days is in her right hand; and in her left hand riches and honour. Her ways are ways of pleasantness, and all her paths are peace.

❖ Luke 9:13-17 But he said unto them, Give ye them to eat. And they said, We have no more but five loaves and two fishes; except we should go and buy meat for all this people. For they were about five thousand men. And he said to his disciples, Make them sit down by fifties in a company. And they did so, and made them all sit down. Then he took the five loaves and the two fishes, and looking up to heaven, he blessed them, and brake, and gave to the disciples to set before the multitude. And they did eat, and were all filled: and there was taken up of fragments that remained to them twelve baskets.

SELF-REFLECTION

Questions to ask yourself:

1. Think about a time you gave and was so generous that you gave what you did not even have to give. How did you feel? What did you do?

2. In retrospect, what would you do moving forward?

CHAPTER 3

House or God: Believe or Not?

O KAY, SO THIS is a tough one to share, but here it goes. We worked hard to earn money, to buy a house and to keep it. We went into debt to fix it up and to keep it. Now here was the thought, floating around in my mind: sell the house.

After twenty-two years of some good and not so good memories, were we really being asked to let go of the house we have called home for so long?! There was not a lot of emotional strength and faith in what I believed God was asking and saying for us to do. I was not sure if it was the enemy's plan or my own thoughts or God really saying and asking us to sell the house. All I did know is that we needed prayer and so I began to pray.

I prayed three times. First, because there was unbelief from both my husband and me. You see, I had started out with a prayer for help to clean up the clutter and mess I made while going through a season of anxiety and depression. I thought I was specific. It turned out I was not. Therefore, something happened triggering the thought that it was time to sell. I shared the words with my husband, and he doubted, so I prayed again asking God, "Are we to sell the house?" and for a sign that we were supposed to. Well, the same thing that happened before happened again.

Guess what, there was still unbelief even after the trauma of what took place both times before, my husband still doubted. Thus, I went into prayer a third time. This time asking God to show my husband and have him come to realize it was indeed time for us to let the house go. And you know what, God did just that but with the same action that took place before. So after three floods and much debt afterwards, we began the process of selling the house.

I believed this was a test of our faith. Who was our God? Were we trusting in things over the only true God, the creator of Heaven and Earth? Or were we laying up treasures upon this earth that we cannot take with us when we pass away leaving the flesh to turn back to dust? Were we going to serve mammon or God? Were we going to let the house be an idol?

With this testimony, we have lived out the experience for ourselves of having to let something that we value go. We did not have to live vicariously through only hearing about others' loss of a home due to tragedy or financial burden. We experienced the hurt and the brokenness for ourselves. It caused a lot of emotional distance between us. There was disappointment, unbelief, fear, mental trauma, and grief from the loss.

All those emotions rushed in. But God still provided through it all. Not as we had hoped, but as a lesson for us to learn to appreciate what we have and not let it become bigger than Him. For to know that He is God alone and nothing should be before Him. Thank you, Father, for getting us through that emotional roller coaster and teaching us about building heavenly treasures that are eternal and not acquiring earthly treasures that are temporary.

REFERENCE SCRIPTURES

❖ Matthew 6:19-21 Lay not up for yourselves treasures upon the earth, where moth and rust doth corrupt, and where thieves break through and steal: But lay up for yourselves treasures in heaven, where neither moth nor rust doth corrupt, and where thieves do not break through to steal:
For where your treasure is, there will your heart be also.

❖ Matthew 6:24 No man can serve two masters: for either he will hate the one, and love the other; or else he will hold to the one, and despise the other. Ye cannot serve God and mammon.

❖ Exodus 20:1-6 And God spake all these words, saying, I am the Lord thy God, which have brought thee out of the land of Egypt, out of the house of bondage. Thou shalt have no other gods before me. Thou shalt not make unto thee any graven image, or any likeness of any thing that is in heaven above, or that is in the earth beneath, or that is in the water under the earth: Thou shalt not bow down thyself to them, nor serve them: for I the Lord thy God am a jealous God, visiting the iniquity of the fathers upon the children unto the third and fourth generations of them that hate me; And shewing mercy unto thousands of them that love me, and keep my commandments.

SELF-REFLECTION

Questions to ask yourself:

1. Think of a time when God asked you to let something or someone go. How did you feel?

2. Did you let go? If yes, how did you respond to having to let go? If no, why are you still holding on to what you were asked to let go? Are you going to be obedient?

_____

_____

_____

_____

_____

_____

_____

_____

_____

_____

CHAPTER 4

Boast and You Have Your Reward

L ITTLE DID I know that it was boasting and pride when I discussed with others about what I did for people or what I would not do to hurt others. What a way to open a window for the enemy, to allow myself to be tested. The things I did for others should have been kept secret. I should not have said what I would not do or what I would do because I was put in a situation where I did a thing I said I would not do. Who am I to boast of such things? Oh, what pride!

You see, when you boast or show pride, you have your reward. I learned this when I read Matthew 6:1 "Take heed that ye do not your alms before men, to be seen of them: otherwise ye have no reward of your Father which is in heaven." Thus, I believe I was put in a place where I could not help others as a consequence, hence my debt: money in, money out to my debtors. That "robbing Peter to pay Paul" situation I spoke about earlier.

I am so grateful that God has taught me that it is by His grace and mercy that we do well and not of ourselves. For in the flesh, there dwells no good thing. Even when we think to do good, evil is present, so I too, like Paul, thank God through Christ Jesus, our Lord who delivered me from the body of death and sin, that I try my best to bring all requests to Him and seek His will and not my own. I thank God for teaching me, and Jesus for leading me by His Spirit to walk after the things of the Spirit and not after the flesh.

All glory to God, the Father. Hallelujah.

REFERENCE SCRIPTURES

❖ Proverbs 11:2 When pride cometh, then cometh shame: but with the lowly is wisdom.

❖ Matthew 6:1-4 Take heed that ye do not your alms before men, to be seen of them: otherwise ye have no reward of your Father which is in heaven. Therefore when thou doest thine alms, do not sound a trumpet before thee, as the hypocrites do in the synagogues and in the streets, that they may have glory of men. Verily I say unto you, They have their reward. But when thou doest alms, let not thy left hand know what thy right hand doeth: That thine alms may be in secret: and thy father which seeth in secret himself

❖ Romans 7:18 For I know that in me (that is, in my flesh,) dwelleth no good thing: for to will is present with me; but how to perform that which is good I find not.

❖ Ephesians 2:8-9 For by grace are ye saved through faith; and that not of yourselves: it is the gift of God: Not of works, lest any man should boast.

SELF-REFLECTION

Questions to ask yourself:

1. Think of a time when you boasted about something you had done or would not do. How did you feel afterwards?

2. What did you learn from the outcome?

3. What will you do moving forward?

_____

_____

_____

_____

_____

_____

_____

_____

_____

_____

CHAPTER 5

Set Apart

AT ANOTHER POINT in my life, people whom I thought were to remain in my life—friends and family—had begun to distance themselves from me. No reason given. Unanswered telephone calls. No visits to check on me. No more lunch or dinner dates. Others who did answer when I called, the conversations seemed to turn for the worse. Miscommunication and misunderstandings were all that seemed to be in the air. Some words were intentional, others were not. Offense set in. Brokenness set in.

But God, once again, used those moments to draw me closer to Him, in Christ Jesus. Of course, at the time, I did not know that was His plan. He used it for His good. To heal my brokenness and to bind up my wounds. To remind me that He alone is the author and finisher of my faith.

See, my faith was in others. I looked to them to bring me joy and happiness. I looked to them for fulfillment. Without me even knowing it, I had created those who distance themselves from me as idols. Sidebar: At this point, I have to stop and remind us that there should be no other Gods before our Creator. He is a jealous God.

Okay, I am back. You see, God needed me set apart for His purpose and will to be done in my life. Thus, people had to be removed or set apart for a time so that God could begin the good work in me which He started and continues until the day of Christ Jesus.

Glory to the Father. All praises and honor to Him. Thank you for the washing, cleaning, and healing process. Thank you for revealing to me that no one or thing should come before you or be placed above you. Thank you for your generous love, mercy, and grace which are sufficient for the day. In Jesus' name, I pray.

Amen.

REFERENCE SCRIPTURES

❖ Psalms 4:3 But know that the Lord hath set apart him that is godly for himself: the Lord will hear when I call unto him.

❖ Psalms 147:3 He healeth the broken in heart, and bindeth up their wounds.

❖ Philippians 1:6 Being confident of this very thing, that he which hath begun a good work in you will perform it until the day of Jesus Christ

❖ Hebrews 12:2 Looking unto Jesus the author and finisher of our faith; who for the joy that was set before him endured the cross, despising the shame, and is set down at the right hand of the throne of God.

❖ Ecclesiastes 3:1-8 To every thing is a season, and a time to every purpose under the heaven: A time to be born, and a time to die; a time to plant, and a time to pluck up that which is planted; A time to kill, and a time to heal; a time to break down, and a time to build up; A time to weep, and a time to laugh; a time to mourn, and a time to dance; A time to cast away stones, and a time to gather stones together; a time to embrace, and a time to refrain from embracing; A time to get, and a time to lose; a time to keep, and a time to cast away; A time to rend, and a time to sew; a time to keep silence, and a time to speak; A time to love, and a time to hate; a time of war, and a time of peace.

SELF-REFLECTION

Questions to ask yourself:

1. Think of a time when you had no one to turn to and felt alone. What emotions would you describe experiencing at that moment?

2. Feeling excluded, how did you handle your circumstances?

3. Did you turn to other things or people? What was the outcome?

_____

_____

_____

_____

_____

_____

_____

_____

_____

_____

CHAPTER 6

Charged

D URING A SEASON when I read God's word (The Bible) more, went to church more, and prayed a little more, I received a message of encouragement. I was seeking my purpose in Christ Jesus. I wanted understanding. I wanted wisdom and knowledge of the One who could show someone so much love, someone like me—a sinner—who He called, saved, and redeemed by His blood shed on a cross for me, you, and you too.

As I was at work one day, a woman came to me. She said that God sent her to me. She said that He told her to anoint me with oil and tell me that "I am charged." She said she did not know what it meant, but she wanted to be obedient to what God asked her to do. Later, in my reflection, because I did not understand what she meant either, I turned to God's word in the Bible. See, God knew that I was going to search for an answer from Him. He created me to be a searcher for discernment, understanding, and knowledge that only He can provide.

And, wow! What I found was a truth that only He can reveal. What a charge He gave me, the responsibility to go and teach others what He had taught me. Yes, someone like me. I felt so unworthy and unequipped, but with more training from the Holy Spirit, I learned that God uses whom He deems worthy and called. What a wonderful God we serve!

As my mind and heart changed with the work of the Holy Spirit, I knew this was God's purpose for me. He saved me so that I could be used as a disciple for Him, a vessel for His glory and will. I am so ever thankful and grateful to be found worthy by our Creator, I Am That I Am, the Alpha and Omega, Abba Father. Thank you, God, for choosing me and finding me worthy to be used by you. In Jesus' name, I pray. Amen.

Thus, this is how this book came to be. All glory and honor to God, our Father in Heaven. I am charged to share what He has done for me, my family, and others connected to me (known and unknown). Although I sometimes still feel, "Why me?" I know it is for my good and the good of others to be obedient, take up my cross, bear it, and follow after Jesus Christ, our Lord and Savior. For this is why we were created: for His good pleasure. What a blessing to serve God and others according to His will and purpose for us. Life is so much better when you are obedient. Thank you, Jesus. Thank you, Holy Spirit. Thank you, Abba Father, for choosing me.

REFERENCE SCRIPTURES

❖ 2 Timothy 4:1-6 I charge thee therefore before God, and the Lord Jesus Christ, who shall judge the quick and the dead at his appearing and his kingdom; Preach the word; be instant in season, out of season; reprove, rebuke, exhort with all longsuffering and doctrine. For the time will come when they will not endure sound doctrine; but after their own lusts shall they heap to themselves teachers, having itching ears; And they shall turn away their ears from the truth, and shall be turned unto fables. But watch thou in all things, endure afflictions, do the work of an evangelist, make full proof of thy ministry.

❖ Hebrew 13:20-21 Now the God of peace, that brought again from the dead our Lord Jesus, that great shepherd of the sheep, through the blood of the everlasting covenant, Make you perfect in every good work to do his will, working in you that which is well pleasing in his sight, through Jesus Christ; to whom be glory for ever and ever. Amen.

❖ Romans 9:11, 16,-17 (For the children being not yet born, neither having done any good or evil, that the purpose of God according to election might stand, not of works, but of him that calleth;) So then it is not of him that willeth, nor of him that runneth, but of God that sheweth mercy. For the scripture saith unto Pharaoh, Even for this same purpose have I raised thee up, that I might shew my power in thee, and that my name might be declared throughout all the earth.

❖ Exodus 4:10-12 And Moses said unto the Lord, O my Lord, I am not eloquent, neither heretofore, nor since thou hast spoken unto thy servant: but I am slow of speech, and of a slow tongue. And the Lord said unto him, Who hath made man's mouth? or who maketh the dumb, or deaf, or the seeing, or the blind?

have not I the Lord? Now therefore go, and I will be with thy mouth, and teach thee what thou shalt say.

❖ Matthew 16:24-25 Then said Jesus unto his disciplines, If any man will come after me, let him deny himself, and take up his cross, and follow me. For whosoever will save his life shall lose it; and whoso ever will lose his life for my sake shall find it.

❖ Isaiah 43:1, 7, 10-12, 21 But now thus saith the Lord that created thee, O Jacob, and he that formed thee, O Israel, Fear not: for I have redeemed thee, I have called thee by name; thou art mine. Even everyone that is called by my name: for I have created him for my glory, I have formed him; yea, I have made him. Yea are my witnesses, saith the Lord, and my servant whom I have chosen: that ye may know and believe me, and understand that I am he: before me there was no God formed, neither shall be after me. I, even I, am the Lord; and beside me there is no saviour. I have declared, and have saved, and I have shewed, when there was no strange god among you: therefore ye are my witnesses, saith the Lord, that I am God. This people have I formed for myself; they shall shew forth my praise.

❖ Ephesians 3:7-8 Wherefore I was made a minister, according to the gift of the grace of God given unto me by the effectual working of his power. Unto me, who am less than the least of all saints, is this grace given, that I should preach among Gentiles the unsearchable riches of Christ;

❖ Ephesians 4:7-8, 11-12 But unto every one of us is given grace according to the measure of the gift of Christ. Wherefore he saith, When he ascended up on high, he led captivity captive, and gave gifts unto men. And he gave some, apostles; and some, prophets; and some, evangelists; and some, pastors and teachers; For the perfecting of the saints, for the work of the ministry, for the edifying of the body of Christ:

SELF-REFLECTION

Questions to ask yourself-

1. Is there a time when God sent someone to prophesy to you? If so, what did you do?

2. Did you test the spirit against God's living word (the Bible)? Did their words align to God's words for your life?

3. If you haven't experienced this yet, I advise you to begin to journal when it does happen and try the spirit with what God's word say about what was spoken

_____

_____

_____

_____

_____

_____

_____

_____

_____

CHAPTER 7

Charity Better Known as Love

YEARS HAVE PASSED. People have come and gone. Time waits for no one. And yet, here is love. It remains. Like hope and faith, but it is the greatest of all three.

This section is a reflection on 1 Corinthians 13:1-8, 13 and how I meditated on it for revelation in my own life. So before reading my testimony let's read the scripture to set the atmosphere of receiving and understanding: *"though I speak with the tongues of men and angels, and have not charity, I am become as sounding brass, or a tinkling cymbal. And though I have the gift of prophecy, and understand all mysteries, and all knowledge; and though I have all faith, so that I could remove mountains, and have not charity, I am nothing. And though I bestow all my goods to feed the poor, and though I give my body to be burned, and have not charity, it profiteth me nothing. Charity suffereth long, and is kind; charity envieth not; charity vaunteth not itself, is not puffed up, Doth not behave itself unseemly, seeketh not her own, is not easily provoked, thinketh no evil; Rejoiceth not in iniquity, but rejoiceth in the truth; Beareth all things; believeth all things, hopeth all things, endureth all things. Charity never faileth: And now bideth faith, hope, charity, these three; but the greatest of these is charity."*

"Wow" was the only thing I could say after my reflection. Other words were not yet formed. With understanding and knowledge, sometimes all that you can say is nothing because you do not have any other words to describe what reading such truth brings. Your breath is taken away for a moment. Thanks be to God that now I know how powerful the four-letter word love is. Many of us use it so loosely, as if it were just a small noun. Love is not only a noun; it is also a verb, an action word. Love is what you do or show. It is not just an intense feeling or great interest in someone or something.

Do me a favor…read verses 4-8a again. After reading it again, did it make you think, have I loved like this before? How many times in your life can you say you truly loved others like this? Can you think of anyone? I know I am guilty of not showing, giving, or doing love as described in Corinthians, especially during difficult times; it does not come easy at all, without the help of the Holy Spirit.

This is what Jesus did for us. He loves us like this. I am grateful that Jesus did and does what no other person or thing could, by giving up His life as a sacrifice for us, so that we can be set free from our own prisons and miry muck. Such love, to take on the sins of others so that they can live an eternal life. God, my God. Thank you, Jesus. He modeled what love is. How we should not hold people's wrongs against them and that we should bear with others with long-suffering. We should not be provoked to do evil or even think of it. Oh, Lord, forgive me for holding on to offenses and not forgiving with my whole heart. Forgive me for envying and provoking others.

Dear reader, if you by chance are someone I have wronged, please forgive me for such actions. I pray that God helps us to remove such unforgiveness and envying, as far as the east is from the west from our hearts and minds so that we can truly live free. For you see, it gains us nothing but misery and sorrow. Let us strive to love as described in 1 Corinthians 13 and as Christ modeled for us. Thank you, Jesus, for loving us with such powerful and great love. Praises, glory, and all honor belong to you. In your precious name, I pray, Jesus. Amen.

REFERENCE SCRIPTURES

- ❖ John 3:16 For God so loved the world, that he gave his only begotten Son, that whosever believeth in him should not perish, but have everlasting life.
- ❖ Matthew 6:14-15 For if ye forgive men their trespasses, your heavenly Father will forgive you: But if ye forgive not men their trespasses, neither will your Father forgive your trespasses.
- ❖ Psalms 103:12 As far as the east is from the west, so far hath he removed our transgressions from us.
- ❖ Matthew 18:21-22 Then came Peter to him, and said, Lord, how oft shall my brother sin against me, and I forgive him? till seven times? Jesus saith unto him, I say not unto thee, Until seven times: but, Until seventy times seven.
- ❖ 1 John 4:16, 19 And we have known and believed the love that God hath to us. God is love; and he that dwelleth in love dwelleth in God, and God in him. We love him, because he first loved us.

SELF-REFLECTION

Questions to ask yourself:

1. How would you describe the four letter word- love?

2. After reading 1 Corinthians 13, did you think about have you loved like that before or how many times in your life can you say you truly loved others like that?

3. Did you think about how many times have you forgiven or not forgiven someone for something they have said or done? What does Jesus say about love and forgiveness?

_____

_____

_____

_____

_____

_____

_____

_____

_____

CHAPTER 8

Only One Tenth So Dollar Up

EARLIER IN THIS book, I wrote about giving to others and falling into a ditch. Here I am being tested to trust God with my finances, even while in my ditch. See, God has answered my prayer of taking my two fish and five loaves (again, my paycheck, in case you are confused) and making it more than enough while I am in debt. But, I was supposed to still give what belongs to Him—the ten percent, the first fruit.

I still have not trusted Him with what really belongs to Him anyway. Thus, the message "dollar up" was what He gave me. See, He wants me to look at it this way: I am being allowed to keep nine-tenths of what He blessed me with, so what is one-tenth? That is all He is asking for. What a gracious God!

Today, I am embarking on a new season of trusting God with my finances by giving the tenth that belongs to Him. I desire to stop robbing Him. I trusted in other things and people, but now it is time to trust in God. To watch Him in all His glory do abundantly more than I can ever ask, all the while trusting Him through my giving. Stay tuned to see how this story unfolds in my life.

REFERENCE SCRIPTURES

❖ Genesis 28:22a and of all that thou shalt give me I will surely give the tenth unto thee.

❖ Proverbs 3:9-10 Honour the LORD with thy substance, and with the firstfruits of all thine increase: So shall thy barns be filled with plenty, and thy presses shall burst out with new wine.

❖ Leviticus 27:30 And all the tithe of the land, whether of the seed of the land, or of the fruit of the tree, is the LORD's: it is holy unto the LORD.

❖ 2 Corinthians 9:6-7 But this I say, He which soweth sparingly shall reap also sparingly; and he which soweth bountifully shall reap also bountifully. Every man according as he purposeth in his heart, so let him give, not grudgingly, or of necessity: for God loveth a cheerful giver.

❖ Numbers 18:25-28a And the LORD spake unto Moses, saying, Thus speak unto the Levites, and say unto them, When ye take of the children of Israel the tithes which I have given you from them for your inheritance, then ye shall offer up an heave offering of it for the LORD, even a tenth part of the tithe. And this your heave offering shall be reckoned unto you, as though it were the corn of the threshingfloor, and as the fulness of the winepress. Thus ye also shall offer an heave offering unto the LORD of all your tithes, which ye receive of the children of Israel;

❖ Malachi 3:8, 10 Will a man rob God? Yet ye have robbed me. But ye say, Wherein have we robbed thee? In tithes and offerings. Bring ye all the tithes into the storehouse, that there may be meat in mine house, and prove me now herewith, saith the Lord of hosts, if I will not open you the windows of heaven, and pour you out a blessing, that there shall not be room enough to receive it.

SELF-REFLECTION

Questions to ask yourself?

1. Are you robbing God of the whole tenth we are asked to give? If yes, what is keeping you from tithing?

2. Write a plan to how you will begin to give back to what belongs to God any way.

3. Who can help you be accountable to your plan?

_____

_____

_____

_____

_____

_____

_____

CHAPTER 9

Get it Done

HERE I AM, after being charged, yet I have not done what was being asked of me. I have been putting off what is required of me to do.

Why did I not move forward at that time? I guess because I still could not believe that God would choose someone like me. I did not believe I was good enough. I felt unworthy, so I fled like Jonah. That was not being obedient. But thanks to God for His love and care for me, that He was waiting for me to get it done. Twice, maybe more, but definitely twice He spoke for me to get it done, so the "it" is this book. The "it" could be something else, however, until the message is made a little more specific, I am believing the "it" is this book. (Just a sidebar thought. Stay tuned.)

So here, I am taking a step to being obedient because being disobedient causes a lot of unwanted anxiety and stress. I want to be healed and set free, so I am keeping my promise, my vow to share God's word and what He has done for me.

You see, I learned in God's waiting, that He takes those people who are broken and appear unworthy to others, and uses them for His good and glory. Here I was thinking that I was not worthy of anything or something because of things I had done or said, but the Father chose me, predestined me for a time such as this. God, my God!

Here, I was thinking that people did not want to be around me because they thought I was a negative person, and all the while, it was God setting me apart for the washing, cleansing, and teaching, to help me become what He wills for me to be according to His purpose and plans that are good and not of evil. He shared with me many times that nothing can separate me from His love and plans for me. What love that

God shows us in our messiness. He gave up His own son for our sins. Repeatedly, we are reminded of His great love for humankind, which He made in His likeness, so why would I not want to serve Him? He deserves that and much more than I can ever repay. So God, here I am, use me for your glory and honor.

Father God, I thank you for cleaning me from the inside out and choosing to use me, even me. Have your way with me. Jesus, I am yielding and pray that the Holy Spirit helps me to keep your way and precepts because if I am left to my own devices, I fear that I may sin again. Holy Spirit, lead me, guide me, and teach me continually. God, I take cover under your wings. You are my refuge and ever-present help in time of need. I praise your Holy name, Jesus. It is in your name I pray and leave these words for others to learn from your goodness, mercy, and grace. Amen.

Amen.

REFERENCE SCRIPTURE

❖ Romans 8:28-37 And we know that all things work together for good to them that love God, to them who are called according to his purpose. For whom he did foreknow, he also did predestinate to be conformed to the image of his Son, that he might be the firstborn among many brethen. Moreover whom he did predestinate, them he also called: and whom he called, them he also justified: and whom he justified, them he also glorified. What shall we then say to these things? If God be for us, who can be against us? He that spared not his own Son, but delivered him up for us all, how shall he not with him also freely give us all things? Who shall lay any thing to the charge of God's elect? It is God that justifieth. Who is he that condemneth? It is Christ that dies, yea rather, that is risen again, who is even at the right hand of God, who also maketh intercession for us. Who shall separate us from the love of Christ? shall tribulation, or distress, or persecution, or famine, or nakedness, or peril, or sword? As it is written, For thy sake we are killed all the day long; we are accounted as sheep for the slaughter. Nay, in all these things we are more than conquerors through him that loved us.

SELF-REFLECTION

Questions to ask yourself:

1. What is it that God has asked you to do? Have you done it yet? If not, what is keeping you from moving forward?

2. If yes, what have you experienced in being obedient?

3. If you are not sure that God has asked you to do something, begin to reflect on your current emotions and why you might feel the way you feel and what could be the cause of them. You may find the answer is that God asked you to do something, and you didn't so the end result is an underlying issue, per se.

_____

_____

_____

_____

_____

_____

CHAPTER 10

ABC's of Praises to God

HEAVENLY FATHER GOD, I praise you because you are awesome and amazing. You are bold, beautiful, and caring. You are compassionate and divine. You are my defender and encourager. You are efficient and faithful.

I praise you because of your forgiveness of my sins and graciousness to me. You are gentle and humble in your correction and guidance. You are my healer and helper. You are immovable and infinite in your power. You are joy, kindness, and knowledge.

I praise you for being my keeper and being longsuffering with me. You are loving and merciful. Thank you for your nearness and never-ending love. You are omnipresent and omnipotent. You are patient and my provider. You are quintessential and quiet.

I praise you for being my redeemer and my rest. You are sovereign and my savior. You are my teacher and trustworthy. You are understanding and unchanging. You are ubiquitous and victorious.

You are my vindicator and way-maker. You are a wise and wonderful counselor. You are worthy. You are Xristos (Greek for Christ). You are Yahweh. I thank you for your zeal for me.

Thank you for not giving up on me. Thank you for being Emmanuel, God with us. Thank you for being the Alpha and Omega, the Beginning and the End. Thank you for being I AM Who I Am. Thank you for being the Lion of Judah. All honor, glory, and praise belong to you.

I had to take that moment to extend praises to God and give Him all the glory for what He has done in my life thus far and yet to do. He has changed me from glory to glory for His honor and purpose. It is still unimaginable and indescribable how God can love me so much, and not just me but all of us. We are so undeserving and yet He loves us and does so knowing all that we were, are, and will be.

What a mighty God we serve! I thank God for this new creature He created me to be. The old is washed away. (Side note: and if you knew me when, then you know what I am talking about.) Thank God that all things can and do become new again in Christ Jesus, our Lord and Savior.

SELF-REFLECTION

Questions to ask yourself:

1. Think back over your life. How has God changed you? What did He save you from?

2. How have you aknowledged Him for all that He has done and is doing in your life?

3. If you have not acknowledged Him, you can start by creating your own ABC of Praise Prayer.

_____

_____

_____

_____

_____

_____

_____

_____

_____

_____

CONCLUSION

So here it is... If He did it for me, He surely can do it for you too. He can change you from the inside out, turn your ashes into beauty. All you have to do is surrender, or re-surrender if you need to, but do it while He can still be found. Draw close to Him, and He will draw close to you. I am so glad that I did. I am so grateful to the One who loves me because He chose to use me as a vessel to show His glory and goodness to others so they too can be saved.

Here I am, through my writings, reflecting on the breadcrumbs and seeds that God left for me on my faith walk to abide in Him and draw closer to Him so that I can inspire you to continue or begin your walk with the Lord. I promise, it will all be worth it in the end.

I have come to the end of this book. I hope that by reading it, you have picked up a breadcrumb or two and can use them as seeds to help others on your journey. I desire for you to trust in God with all your heart and lean not on your own understanding. (I write this for myself too.) I desire for you to taste and see that the Lord is good by seeking His Kingdom first. You can begin again or start for the first time by repenting and asking for forgiveness as God so freely gives.

Here are some words to help you. I say them with you: Lord, Jesus, I repent of my sins and (re)surrender my life to you. Wash and cleanse me, Father. I believe that Jesus Christ died on the cross for my sins and rose again on the third day for my victory. I believe that in my heart and make confession with my mouth, that Jesus is my Lord and Savior. Amen. Amen. What is next, you ask? Well, here is a plan to follow which should help you to draw closer in your relationship with God.

- ❖ Consider being baptized. This is your wedding day with the Father, the Son, and Holy Spirit.
- ❖ Read the word of God, the Bible as often as you can, daily.
- ❖ Pray as often as you can, daily.

- ❖ Find a church to fellowship with like-minded Christians.
- ❖ Be patient with yourself.
- ❖ Be kind to yourself. It does not happen overnight. Trust me I know. It has taken many lessons, trials, and tribulations to get to this point where I can say to you without a shadow of a doubt that God is real and forever faithful more than anything is or person we know.

Until we meet again, may God bless you, keep you, and make His face to shine upon you.

All praise, glory, and honor to God. For Thine is the Kingdom, and the Power, and the Glory, forever. Amen. Amen.

REFERENCE SCRIPTURES

❖ 2 Corinthians 5:17 Therefore if any man be in Christ, he is a new creature: old things are passed away; behold, all things are become new.

❖ James 4:8 Draw nigh unto God, and he will draw nigh unto you. Cleanse your hands, ye sinners; and purify your hearts, ye double minded.

❖ Isaiah 55:6-9 Seek ye the Lord while he may be found, call ye upon him while he is near: Let the wicked forsake his way, and the unrighteous man his thoughts: and let him return unto the Lord, and he will have mercy upon him; and to our God, for he will abundantly pardon. For my thoughts are not your thoughts, neither are your ways my ways, saith the LORD. For as the heavens are higher than the earth, so are my ways, and thoughts than your thoughts.

❖ Psalms 116:12-19 What shall I render unto the LORD for all his benefits toward me? I will take the cup of salvation, and call upon the name of the LORD. I will pay my vows unto the LORD now in the presence of all his people. Precious in the sight of the LORD is the death of his saints. O LORD, truly I am thy servant; I am thy servant, and the son of thine handmaid: thou hast loosed my bonds. I will offer to thee the sacrifice of thanksgiving, and will call upon the name of the LORD. I will pay my vows unto the LORD now in the presence of all his people, In the courts of the LORD's house, in the midst of thee, O Jerusalem.
Praise ye the LORD.

❖ Proverbs 3:5-6 Trust in the Lord with all thine heart; and lean not unto thine own understanding. In all thy ways acknowledge him, and he shall direct thy paths.

❖ Psalms 34:8 O taste and see that the LORD is good: blessed is the man that trusted in him.

❖ Matthew 6:33 But seek ye first the kingdom of God, and his righteousness; and all these things shall be added unto you.

❖ Numbers 6:24-26 The LORD bless thee, and keep thee: The LORD make his face shine upon thee, and be gracious unto thee: The LORD lift up his countenance upon thee, and give thee peace.

SELF-REFLECTION

Questions to as yourself:

1. Where is your journey with God?

2. Have you accepted Jesus as your Lord and Savior? If not, what is keeping you from taking that next step?

3. Now that you have accpeted Jesus as Lord, and the only way to God, the Father, what is your next level? Write your plan to your next step.

_____

_____

_____

_____

_____

_____

_____

_____

_____

_____

_____

ABOUT THE AUTHOR

Isabel, the second oldest of four siblings, is currently married with a blended family: two sons and three daughters. She was born in Vineland, New Jersey, and raised in Bridgeport, Connecticut.

She served three years in the military with an honorable discharge. She obtained her Master's in Education from Regent University and taught in three Virginia school districts. She obtained her Life Coach certificate from the International Association of Professions Career College.

Through many trials and tribulations, she has come to know Jesus as her Lord and Savior. She rededicated her life to God and desires to do His will and purpose for her life. She now realizes that He has the greater and bett-er plan.

Reader Reviews

One reader stated, *"what I enjoyed about Breadcrumbs and Seeds is the author's transparency. She gave you enough information (breadcrumbs) to make it relatable to your own life experiences. Although she says breadcrumbs and seeds, I see goldenuggets because she provides you with scriptures to guide you through life experiences. I also like how she formatted her book in a journal style giving you the opportunity to write your reflections as it relates to you as a reader."*

A second reader wrote, *"I loved the formatting of this book: the prayers, personal testimony, and scripture. I believe the author is extremely motivated and has found peace through the grace of our Lord and Savior. I know what I'm getting my friends for Christmas, this book! Thank you Isabel, it's very well written and I enjoyed it thoroughly."*

Another reader wrote, *"This book was a page turner for me. I appreciated the message brought forth, the incorporation of God's word and truth. Author, Isabel offers encouraging words how God has guided her in life. What an awesome read. I look forward to the next book. God bless the Author, Isabel for writing and sharing her story. I truly enjoyed "Breadcrumbs and Seeds" May God continue to bless you on your journey, Isabel."*

Printed in the United States
by Baker & Taylor Publisher Services